문안의 여자 문밖의 여자

The Woman Inside The Woman Outside

이 도서의 국립중앙도서관 출판예정도서목록(CIP)은 서지정보유통지원시스템 홈페이지(http://seoji.nl.go.kr)와 국가자료공동목록시스템(http://www.nl.go.kr/kolisnet)에서 이용하실 수 있습니다. (CIP제어번호 : CIP2016006353)

문안의 여자 문밖의 여자

이혜숙 한영(韓英) 시집

글나무

시인의 말

살면서 넘어질 때가 있었습니다
넘어지면서 피 흘림도 닦아가며
고름 맺히는 자리,
새살이 올라오는 것을 지켜보며,
세상사가 훤하게 슬프다는 것도
알았습니다
주제 넘은 욕심인 줄 알면서
영문 번역시집을 내기까지의
많은 생각으로
고심했습니다
아직도 부족한
끝없이 부족한
작은 이 시집으로 상처받은
영혼의 아픈 마음을 다독일 수 있는
치유가 될 수 있다면 좋겠습니다
번역해 주신 이영순 시인님께도
깊이 감사드립니다

2013 폭염에 홀로 떠나신
당신(어머니)을 그리며
2016년 삼월 이혜숙

Poet's Note

While living, there were times when
I tumbled down
Watching the granulation
from the place where
I fell,
wiped the flowing blood and
the puss was formed
I fully understand that
the worldly affairs are bitterly sad
I know I'm impertinent, however
I've mulled over the publication of
this Korean-English poetry book
Though this work is not qualified
I eagerly hope
it will comfort the ached heart of a soul
Thank you to Lee Young-soon
for offering her beautiful translations
Missing my mother who
passed away in the heat all alone in 2013

March 2016
Lee Hye-sook

제1부
어달동 사람들

제2부
마법의 주문

제3부
핫라인 통신

제4부
목관 악기의 일기

제 1 부

어달동 사람들

The Persons at Eodal Village

수족관 숭어

그녀를 보았다. 비린내 질펀한 횟집에서 삶은 끊임없이 흔들리며 헤엄치는데 숨 쉴 줄 모르는 한 마리의 숭어가 생명의 비늘을 떨어뜨리고 있었다. 세상을 헤엄치는 일, 이처럼 무거운 것인가. 지상의 꽃들도 다 젖으며 핀다지만 세상 물고기라고 다 물고기던가. 시샘 속에서 흔들리지 않으려 버둥대지만 깔딱이는 아가미로 숨조차 마음대로 쉬지 못한 죗값을 치르느라 자아를 버려야 했다. 팔다리가 잘리는 고통을 감내하며 그녀는 저 몸의 비늘을 좋아했다. 은빛 비늘을 사랑하기보다 받으려고만 했던 그녀의 몸이 아프기 시작했다. 가릴 것 없는 알몸뚱이가 편안은 했지만 날마다 찔러대는 가시를 뽑기는 어려웠다. 그녀는 아픈 다리를 절뚝이며 삶과 죽음의 경계를 헤엄치기 시작했다. 비늘 반짝이는 은빛 몸으로 살고자 링거를 맞고 있었다. 그녀는 이미 끊어진 숨통이 갇혀버린 수족관에서 제 온몸의 흰 비늘을 지키려 소중한 것을 버려야 했다.

The Mullet in an Aquarium

I saw her. In a raw fish restaurant, the smell of fish swimming constantly, however a mullet who stopped breathing was dropping her scale of life. Swimming through the world. Is it that hard? Though all the flowers on earth open in pain, can we call every fish a real fish? Struggling to stand right in the jealously, she had to abandon her ego as her panting gill couldn't inhale. In spite of the great pain of severed arm and leg, she loved her scale. Her body, not loving her silver scale but being loved by it, began to ache. Her naked body was okay, but pulling the poking fish bone out was difficult. She began to swim at the border of life and death, limping. She had an IV for keeping her silver body with shining scales alive. In the aquarium where her lifeless heart was kept, she had to give up the precious breath to keep her white scale.

나목

잎 떨어진 고욤나무다

세상 겁날 것 없었는데
고개 숙인 채
수식어가 떨어지는 것을
보다

느슨해도 좋을 쉰
나이인데
왜 아직 팽팽함으로
고단한가

저만치 걸어오던 수많은
날들이
마주 대항해도 겁나지
않던 일들이
빗금 간 항아리처럼
두려움 가득하다

때로는
존재하지 않는 일조차
소리 내며 비명으로 터지다

이제 버림의 미학을 아는
나무가 되어
한 걸음 비켜서서
누군가 쉬어 갈 수 있는
그늘을 만들겠다

A Naked Tree

A lotus persimmon tree bare of leaves

I was afraid of nothing, but
I see a change, my head falls

Just in my fifties
A good age for relaxation, yet
why am I tired and tense?

Lots of days walking far away
Lots of things I stand against bravely
I fear them
like a cracked jar

Sometimes
non existing thoughts break into a loud scream

Now I'll become a tree who knows

the esthetics of emptiness and

make a shelter of shade as one step back

닥터피쉬*

젊은 감각이다

도심을 걸어 나오는 맨발이다
오랫동안 굶주린 사내들이 달려들어 마디마다 콕콕
깨물고 있다
쪼아주며 핥아주는 붉은 입술이다
작은 비명 신음처럼 흐르는 수족관
육천여 사내들은 서로 탐하려 몸살이다
네 개의 눈동자가 눈빛을 마주한다
실로 간만에 느껴보는 교류
차이나 출생 친친어* 터키출신 가라루파*는
부드럽기가 서울 태생이다
엄마보다 성숙한 딸은 몸을 틀어 교태를 부린다
건장한 사내들 젊은 딸에게 매달린다
이들은 섭씨 28도의 물에서 잘 견딜 수 있지만
미세한 파문에 상처를 입고 콩새만한 가슴 두근거린다
천천히 옮기는 발 간지럽다
나를 누가 이처럼 사랑할 수 있는가

곳곳이 아픈 나를 누가 치유할 수 있는가
연못처럼 좁은 병원 나무부스에 앉아
시린 가슴 다 고쳐 퇴원 수속을 밟았다

발가락이 봄이다

* 친친어, 가라루파는 물고기 이름이며 닥터피시는 각질을 갉아먹는 물고기 이다.

Doctor Fish

Young sense

Barefoot walking from downtown
Hungry guys rush and bite every joint
Red lips pecking and licking
In the aquarium, low screams stream like moaning
Six thousand men are dying for lust
The glitter of four eyes are met
Such a feeling of consensus
Joe fish from China
Garra rufa from Turkey
They are soft and fair like Seoulite
A daughter more mature than her mother plays the coquette
Robust guys hang around
They can endure the 28 degree centigrade water, but
the scratches caused by the ripplet
make their tiny hearts pound hard
They tickle my moving feet

Who could love me like this

Who could cure every part of my ached body

Sitting on a wooden booth in a small clinic, I

fill the form of discharge because

my lonely heart is cured

Toes are spring

춤추는 여자

그녀는 스페인의 플라맹고다. 춤에 매료된 그녀 집시 춤을 추는 불꽃이다. 아름다운 선율 춤에 사로잡힌 관능적인 몸짓, 손뼉 소리에 슬픈 가락으로 춤추는 생명력 불어넣는 열꽃이다. 춤추다 땅에 묻힌 연인 아르헨티나의 애인이다. 역동적인 춤 독보적인 모습 카르멘이다. 예견할 수 없는 불 밝은 창으로 바뀌던 잠재된 끼 그녀만의 탁월한 재능이다. 피토스*로 멋을 내고 팔마스*로 박자 맞추는 치맛자락 펄럭일 때, 그녀는 이미 주목받는 한 사람의 무용수다. 스텝 소리가 무대를 흔들며 정열의 도가니로 열기를 뿜는 땀, 흥건한 그녀는 삶의 돌파구를 찾아 공연을 펼치는 일명 은영 엄마다.

* 피토스 : 손가락으로 소리내기
* 팔마스 : 손뼉 치며 박자 맞추기

A Dancing Woman

She's Spain's Flammence. Being fascinated by dance, she's a flame of Gypsy dance. Beautiful melody. The sensual pose captured by dance. A lively fever dancing in a sad tune with a clapping audience. A love buried while dancing. Argentina's love. Energetic dance. Unrivaled figure, Carmen. Her unpredictable innate talent. It's an excellent gift of her own. As she amplifies with phytos*, keeps time with Palmas* and flaps her skirt, she comes in the spotlight. The sound of her steps trembles the stage and turns it into a crucible of passion. The radiating sweat. Made sweat. She dances for a living. Her nickname is Eunyoung's mom.

* phytos : Making sound with fingers
* palmas : Keeping time by clapping

관계

뇌성마비 장애를 지닌 불쌍한
남자를 혼자 보내고
돌아서 눈물을 훔치는 여자의
설운 심정을 훔쳐보았다
휘청거리며 취한 듯 길을 걷고 있는 두 사람의
관계는 끊어질 수 없는 필연이었다
끝내 밀어낼 수 없는 관계가 여자의 상처로 전해져
장애를 지닌 남자의 걸음이 자꾸만 술에 취한 듯
떠내려가는 듯 보였다
나는 멀어지는 남자의 어깨가 가늘게 떨고 있는 것을
어머니가 된 심정으로 훔쳐보고
강물 위로 떠다니는 꽃잎처럼 섧게만 울어 주었다
단순하다고 치부하는 남들의 시선도 아랑곳없었다
두 사람의 어려운 관계만이 서럽도록 안타까워 홀로
눈가를 훔치곤 했다
취한 듯 휘청거리며 떠내려가던 남자는
뒤돌아보며 뒤틀리는 입으로 말을 했다
때론 빨리 가기도 하고

때론 늦게 가기도 하고
가만히 서서 기다리고 싶다고
그렇게 말하는 남자의 어깨가 한없이 작아 보였다
이것이 두 사람의 관계였다.

The Relationship

I peeped into the sorrowful heart of a
woman who wiped her eyes after
sending a cerebral palsied man alone
The relationship between the two, a wasted gait,
was an inevitable continuity
As if the relationship she couldn't sever became her scar
his walking seemed to be swept away like a drunkard
Far away
I peeped his shoulders trembling softly
as if I were his mother and
cried like floating petals on the river
I didn't mind other's concerns
Their hard situation made me wipe my eyes alone helplessly
The staggering man turned back and said
with his twisted mouth
Sometimes he'd like to go fast
Sometimes he'd like to go late
Quietly he'd like to wait standing

When he said this

his shoulders seemed so small

That's the relationship of the two

칸나의 유혹

당신에게 나는 늦게 피고 싶은 꽃이었습니다
늦은 꽃이란 걸 알았을 때 당신께 멀리로 잃어진 사람이었습니다
지금 우리는 같은 길을 가고 있습니다
제 몸에 상처 하나씩 지닌 채
애써 조금씩 보듬으며 칸나의 입술처럼 떨고 있는 것을 보았습니다
곪아버린 물집이 손톱 끝으로 만져지기만 해도 곧 핏물로 터져버릴 것 같아
그저 한쪽이 말 없어야 했습니다

다가서는 그대를 밀어내는 것 결코 쉽지 않았습니다
다가서면 설수록 달게 삼키고 싶은 욕심에 가슴은 무속인의
춤사위처럼 쿵쿵 소리를 냈습니다
어깨가 조금씩 흘러내릴 때 입술은 타고 있었지만 제 심장 소리에 아파할 것을
염려하여 속으로 울음 삼켜야 했습니다

붉은 칸나의 열꽃이 불혹의 위기처럼

내 지나간 길을 손가락으로 짚었을 때 붉은 칸나는 피를 토해야만 했습니다.

The Canna's Seduction

For you I was a flower
wishing to bloom late
When I knew it
I was a forgotten man to you
Now we are on the same path
Having a scar on each body,
each saw each tremble, embracing one's scar
like the lips of canna
The festered blister seemed to bleed
with the slightest touch, so
the other had to be speechless

It was hard to push off your approach
The more you came closer,
the stronger the desire of accepting you
made my heart pound like a shaman's dance
Though my shoulders shrunk and my lips parched
I had to swallow my tears

due to my aching heart

When the red eruption of the red canna touched
the crossed path of mine with her fingers
the red canna must vomit blood
like a mid-life crisis

어달동 사람들

하늘을 이고 세상을 살던
언덕배기 마을은 바람에 순종했다

배고픔 가득 머금은 달동네 사람들
하나둘 바다로 마실 가면 어머니의 시린 손
동정 깃처럼 하얗다

하늘 한 자락
바다에 잠겨 소리죽여 울 적마다
식솔들 얼굴
이팝나무 꽃잎으로 흔들렸다

목숨을 담보 삼는 힘든 자맥질
포구에 갈매기 끼룩끼룩대고
그날 바다 빛은 옥색 저고리다

The Persons at Eodal Village

The village on the hill carrying the sky on his head
obeyed the wind

The villagers in a hungry slumI
When they go to sea, every mother's cold hands are
as white as the collar of a Korean coat

Whenever a bit of sky sobs sinking in the sea
the faces of the families tremble like
the blossoms of fringe trees

The hard work of diving insured by life beneath the skin
At the port the sea gulls are honking and
on that day the color of the sea is a jade green jacket

백두산 천지

중생대부터
천지창조의 신비를 간직한
천상호수를 보는 찰나

가슴 터지는 뭉클함이다

원시가 숨을 쉬는 신비의 늪
호수에 하얗게 피어오르는
조팝꽃을 닮은 그림자

그 자리를 떠나지 못하고

분화구에 물 담고 있는
그곳에서 불의 신
프로메테우스를 만났을까
수정궁을 짓고 살고 있는
백장수와 공주는 보았을까

중국 지린성 경계에서
당신은 침묵한 채
아직 다하지 못한 평화의 껍질을 벗기고

The Crater Lake on the Mt. Baekdu

At the moment
I look at the crater lake which mirrors the mystery of Creation
from the Mesozoic Era

I feel a lump in my throat

The mysterious marsh where the Genesis breathes
The shadow resembling bridal wreath blossoms is
misty over the lake

In the crater lake
did you meet Prometheus, god of fire?
Did you happen to see General Paek and a princess
living in a crystal palace?

At the border of the Jirin District of China
you are silent, peeling the skin of unfulfilled peace

제 2 부

마법의 주문

A Magic Chant

밀랍인형

—일본군 위안부

나눔의 집 퇴촌은 열도가 할퀸
자국으로 가득하다

할머니의 한숨 방공호처럼 파여 있다
온몸으로 비벼도 치유할 수 없는
흉터 같은 상처,
서른여섯 해를 차이고 찔린 설움의 골
너무 깊다

할머니는 때밀이 수건으로 밀어보지만
몸뚱이에 박힌 일장기의 문신,
되살아난다

기억을 저장한
열두 살의 상흔 연약한 골수에 뿌리박혀
군화에 밟힌 무궁화는
밤마다 꽃잎을 떨구다

웅크린 밀랍인형
증언을 은폐하려 내리친
제국의 칼끝에 주검이 되지 못한 것이 한스럽다

경기도 광주시 퇴촌면 무수리 65번 뜨락,
꽃잎이 낭자하다

핏빛으로 물든 그 어느 날

A Wax Doll

—The Comfort Woman

The shelter is filled with scratches by Japan

The sigh of a grandma is trenched like a dugout
The scar that can't be removed
by just rubbing hard
The hollow of sorrow kicked and stabbed for 36 years
It's too deep

The grandma scrubs her scars off the body, but
the flag tattoo of Imperialist Japan hangs on,
revives with each pulse

The unforgettable scar of a twelve year old girl is cut
deep into her heart
Every night
the rose of sharon trampled by the combat boots
drops its petals

A crouching wax doll

It's a regret for her not to die by the knife of Imperialist Japan which

muffles the screams

65 Musuri Toechonmyeon, Gwangju, Gyeonggi

Petals are scattered all over

One day soaked in blood

능소화

너는 양반집 규수로 태어났다지
양반집 마당에서만 볼 수 있던 네가
칠월 초여름날 요요하게 웃으며
내 발자국 소리 들으려 귀 활짝
열고 있고나

눈부셔 쳐다볼 수 없는 너
네 등에 업혀 사랑노래 불렀을 때
뱀처럼 똬리 틀어
허리 친친 죄어주던 그날
내 독에 눈멀어 영혼마저 상실해도
시공을 뛰어넘는 너와의 사랑에
한 점 후회가 없고나

봉긋한 입 벌려 내 안에
엎드린 물방울들이 널 받아들이고
한낮 붉은 처녀막으로 기화하던 그날
우리가 잡은 손 놓치지 않고

손 흔들며 걸었어야 했는데
끝내 네 꽃가루에 나는 눈멀고
이렇게 멀리 앉아 손 흔들고 있고나

Jacaranda

You, daughter of a noble birth
You, whom we only see
in the yard of nobleman's house
laugh distantly on the summer day of early July and
open all your ears to listen for my gait

You are too bright to see
The day when
I sing the love song on your back
you hold my waist tightly
like a coiled snake
Even if your venom makes me blind and takes my soul
I won't regret our boundless love

On the day when
the water drops in my opened mouth,
accepts you and evaporates
as red hymen

We should have walked holding our hands tightly
But the pollen makes me blind and
I just sit waving from afar

능소화 2

너는 칠월의 피에로다

벼랑을 타고 오르며 아스라한 곡예를 즐기는
어릿광대의 슬픔이다
속 깊은 아픔, 아린 눈물로 피워낸 불꽃이다
모가지 가늘어진 칠흑 같은 밤의 침묵이다
소멸하는 시간 속에서 살아가는 허무의 꽃이다
어둠 속, 숨죽인 고요를 품고 마음 시린 그곳
스스로 가슴 저 끝자락에 뿌리박힌, 발갛게 코 부은 피에로다
살고 있는 세상이 어둠인지라 울음과 웃음으로
가슴 적시며 주황빛 몸짓으로 다가오는
너는 내게 지울 수 없는 불멸의 피에로다
저녁노을로 타고 있는 내 생채기 같은 아픔이다

바람 불고 비 오는 날 눈부시게 흔들리는 시계추다

Jacaranda Ⅱ

You are a pierrot of July

The grief of a clown who enjoys risky stunts climbing the cliff
The deep ache, the flame fed by kerosine tears
The silence of dark night with a thinner neck
The flower of nihil living in the extinguished time
The pierrot with a swollen red nose who
rooted to the end of his chest alone
rooted in the very place of darkness and deadly quiet
You, the immortal pierrot who
comes to me as scarlet gesture
wetting the heart with laughter and crying as
this living world is the darkness
The scratch of ache burning as an evening ember

The bright, swaying pendulum on a windy and rainy day

어머니의 담벼락

담벼락이 골다공증을 앓고 있다
톡, 치면
그대로 무너질 것 같은 담

무릎 관절을 앓는
허기진 시간
간신히 지탱하는 몸
강빛처럼 서늘하다

앙캉한 몸
폭우에 흔들릴 때마다 몸에서 흐르는
시멘트 부스러기

어머니의 관절 마디는
엇박자로 삐걱대다

Mother's Wall

The wall is infected with osteoporosis
Just one tap
it seems to fall

The hungry hour of suffering from arthritis
The poorly operated body is
chilly like a river

The skinny body
A scrap of cement falls
whenever it is trembled by heavy rain

Mother's joints
creak off beat

마법의 주문

—포커

빨아들일 것 같은 어둠의 블랙홀
입장 번호를 받아 쥔 채
인생에 마법을 걸어본다
폼 나게 돌려라
섹시하게 쿨하게
그대의 자궁 속 연어알 같은 머니로 채워줄
몽환의 바다에 나가 비키니 벗어 던진 마법의 주문
뛰어라 뛰다가 넘다가 파도 타다가 자빠져라
외롭고 외로워서
숨넘어가도록 사랑한 마법에 걸린
실성한 여자
후드득후드득
소나기 지나가고 칠칠 거리는 눈비는
습하게 오고
파랗게 흔들리는 불빛 속 여자여 쿨하게 출석해라
정동진을 지나 사북을 거쳐 그곳엔 글렌굴드의 연주가 있다
그녀만의 철학이 있다
뭉크의 회화, 아마니체나, 아리스토텔레스, 이지적 광기가 있다

그래 외로우니까 사람이다
사유의 극한으로 몰고 간 형벌, 지더라도 폼 나게
이기면 쿨하게 포커마초의 로망이 있다
뚜 뚜 뚜 뚜뚜 급박한 신호음 자동인출기 앞
"수화기를 바로 놓아 주세요."
아플 만큼 아파야 떨어지는 감기처럼 카지노의 밤은
알라딘의 램프로 마법의 주문처럼 가물거리고 있다.

A Magic Chant

—Poker

The sucking black hole of darkness
I practice magic in my life, holding an entrance
Turn charmingly, sexily and stylishly
The magic chant of taking off your bikini in the fantastic sea that
you'll fill with money that
resembles the eggs of salmon in your womb
Run, run, cross over, surf and then fall
She's so lonely that she's caught by
the magic of deadly love
The insane woman
The shower is over. It is sleeting and humid
You, the woman in the trembling blue light,
attend there charmingly
Passing Jeongdongjin and Sabuk, you can see Glangeuld's performance
She has a philosophy of her own
Munch's picture, Amanichina, Aristotle, there is an intellectual

madness

As we are lonely, we are human

The penalty of extreme thinking, the poker macho's roman:

losing stylishly and winning charmingly

beep-beep-beep-beep urgent signals sound in front of the ATM

"Please hang up the phone."

Like a cold we recover after a long sickness the night of gambling

flickers like the magic chant of Aladdin's lamp

복수초

—눈 속의 꽃

세상 속
꿋꿋이 피었노라
비바람 흔들어도 부서지지 않은 채
보란 듯 길을 갔어라

살다 보면
마음을 베이고
가슴을 다쳤어도 툭툭 털고
눈보라에 복수초로 일어섰노라

때로는 거친 풍랑을 만나 휩쓸리고
찢겨질지라도 괴성을 지르는 유령으로 살고 싶지는 않았노라

세상 속
나는 꿋꿋이 피었노라
눈보라를 헤치고 가고 있는 이 길도
내가 있기 때문이라
나를 생각하는 내가 있기 때문이라.

An Adonis

—The Flower in the Snow

In the world
it bloomed firmly
It marched without any broken part
in the rainstorm

Though she was hurt and
her heart was shut down
she stood against it as an adonis in the snow storm

Sometimes she was swept away and torn in the heavy sea,
but
she didn't accept the life of a screaming ghost

In the world
I bloom firmly
The way I go against the snowstorm
can only exist as I am here
Because it is I who cares for me dearly

강원랜드
—카지노의 밤

1
어느 흐린 날
S시인과 M교수 L여사는 사북 424로 향했다
백운산 해발 1,150미터 청정고원 쩐의 도시로 탈바꿈된
폼생폼사의 행진

처음엔 기차를 타보기 위한 여행
빨려 들어가는 중독이다
파키스탄에서 나오는 천연음이온
암염을 쪼이려는 기대감으로 만삭의 통장 쌓다
노름빛에 쫓겨 막장까지 간 사람들의 마음 틈사이로
한 눈동자가 반짝이다

피로가 암덩이로 몰려오다
도·박·중·독
"더 이상 게임이 아닙니다."
"가까이 오지 마셔요 당신은 이곳에 올 여자가 아닙니다."
인생의 배팅을 게임에 걸고 체험을 맛보기 위한 무단외출

기계와의 싸움은 무모함이 따르는 위험이다

빚더미 속의 실랑이로 모여든 사람들
엥~엥~엥
소방차가 오다
쩐의 전쟁을 방불케 하다.

2
에스컬레이터를 타고 게임장에서 이층 카지노 카페라이터에 오르다
영업 안내판을 보는 그녀는 천연 희석으로 구르고 싶어 한다
백운산 정상 마운틴 탑 1340미터가 미끄러져 내려오다
아찔한 슬롯머신 바카라게임 블랙잭 나는 20배팅이다
회전식 레스토랑에서의 식사 한번 못한 소액 칩이
앵벌이로 변한다. 돌아갈 티켓이 없다
숭숭 구멍 뚫린 주머니가 창피하게 웃고 있다. 값 비싼 해외 관광이다
마운틴 탑에서 내려다본 풍광 황량하다

잃어버린 머니가 마이너스 통장의 초조함으로 곤두박질해 댄다

옆 사람은 대박 그녀는 구멍 뚫린 빈털터리 그래도 "당신은 오지 마셔요"

이런 곳에 올 여자가 아닙니다

병풍처럼 펼쳐진 산봉우리의 운해가 저만치서 부끄러운 미소를 보낸다.

Kangwon Land
—The Night of Casino

1

On a cloud day
Poet S, professor M and Mrs. L left for 424
Sabuk, which is transformed as the city of money on
Mt. Baekun, 1150m high
A vanity march in the air

At first it's just a train trip, but
it becomes an unavoidable addiction
The natural negative ion from Pakistan
With an expectation of exposed to rock salt they
pile up contracting bank books
Between the aching hearts of the gamblers in debt
the apple of an eye glitters

Like a chunk of cancer, fatigue rushes to me
Gambling addiction
"No more games."

"Don't come closer. You don't belong here."
An absence without leave for betting a life
on a gamble
The struggle with a machine is just a reckless challenge

The on-lookers, the fight of penniless gamblers
Weee-oooo Weee-oooo
The fire engine is coming
The scene resembles a money war

2

I get on the escalator to go up to the cafe
A woman looking at the sign board wants to roll
as a native rock
The peak of Mt. Baekun at 1340m slides down
I bet 20 on the Black Jack
Without any chance of eating at a revolving restaurant
the cheap chip changes into a beggar

No ticket to go back
A shameful empty pocket laughs
It's an expensive overseas trip
The view from the mountain top is desolate

Lost money in the wind, nose diving with an anxiousness
of a red bank book

My neighbor hit the Jack Pot
She's penniless. Even so, "Don't come here."
"You don't belong here."
The sea of clouds over the range
calls me back shyly

소리 깊은 가을

별빛과 다투어 쏟아지는
귀뚜라미 소리

은빛 날개 달고
파랗게 솟아오르는
고추잠자리의
여린 숨결에서 가을이 깊어 가다

코스모스의 한들거리는 연보랏빛 수줍음
황금벌판에 익어 가는
벼들의 물결
켜켜이 쌓이는 마음속

찾아오는 빛깔
가을의 빛깔.

The Autumn of Deep Sound

The sound of a cricket is falling
competing with shining stars

The autumn deepens
in the soft breath of
a red dragonfly
flying high with silver wings

The lilac shyness of a swaying cosmos
The wave of rice
in the golden rice paddy
The inside of a pile of mind

The coming color
The color of autumn

촛불

네가 흔들릴 때마다
나 또한 흔들리고 싶다
제가 젖고 싶을 때
젖은 사람의 색깔로 남아
사람의 빛깔로 적시고 싶다

The Candlelight

Whenever you tremble
I'd like to tremble, too.
Whenever I want to get wet
I'd like to remain in a wet person's color and
be soothed by the colors of humanity

제 3 부

핫라인 통신

Hot Line Communication

달마 스케치

속눈썹 치켜세워 노려보는 눈빛
오금이 저리다 관솔 목각 달마도
화선지에 먹빛으로 휘갈긴 달마도

과녁을 벗어난 생각, 목울대를
조여오는 듯하다
번뇌의 껍질을 쪼아대며 마치
진실을 규명하듯
검게 태운 입술, 번뇌의 올가미에서
풀려나고 있다

한점 바람이 새벽을 앉히고
기억의 저편을 용서할 때
가슴 속
빗살무늬가 지워지고 있다
해탈을 꿈꾸며
흙 냄새 나는 마음꽃 모종을 한다.

The Dharma Sketch

The piercing eyes with upturned eyelashes
An intimidating picture of wooden Dharma sculpture
A brush stroked black Dharma sketch on a Chinese drawing paper

The thought out of lines
seems to press my neck
Pecking the skin of agony, as if to prove the truth,
the black burnt lips of the Dharma picture are
freed from the noose of anguish

When a bit of wind calms the dawn and forgives
the memory beyond
the slant pattern in my heart is erased
Dreaming of deliverance from the ties of the earth
I plant a muddy flower of birth

해가 정동진을 벗기고

그만의 공법으로 축축한 어둠을 휘두르다
날것을 가슴의 불로 익히기엔 역부족이었는지
알몸은 튕겨져 나가다 무엇이든

다 이룰 수 있는 것처럼 혼자 알아 하는 듯
아랫배를 타고 오를 식욕을 느끼더니
살결 부딪는 온기 채 가시기 전 마음 빈틈으로
무작정 허무가 스멀거리고 있다

그때, 바다의 어둠을 다스리던 야경
바람으로 풍화되고 정동진 어느 후미진 그곳

누군가가 절규하는 비명소리 반쯤 벗겨진 해에
젖어, 붉은 파도에 일렁이고 있다

한순간 어둠을 타고
타닥타닥 자작나무 타던 소리
고무풍선 같은 심장

톡톡 찔러대고
눈꺼풀 내려앉는 피로가 바다에 빠진 해처럼
발가벗은 채
언덕 너머 심곡에서 길을 묻는 신음으로
환하게 울렸다

And the Sun Strips Jeongdongjin

He brandishes the wet darkness his own way, but it's beyond
his capacity to cook the raw thing
with the heat of his bosom
His naked body is bounced. As if

he could accomplish everything for himself, he
feels an appetite coming from his lower stomach
Before the warmth on his skin vanishes
nihil creeps through the crack in his mind

Then the night view controlling the dark of the sea
is weathered as the wind, and
at the cove in Jeongdongjin somebody's
shrieking scream, wetted by the half stripped sun,
is rocking on the red wave

In an instant, the sound of burning birch in the dark

is pricking a rubber ballon like heart
The weariness with heavy eyelids
is naked like the sunken sun and
is moaning, asking the way on the hill of Simgok

삼월에 내리는 눈

샤갈의 마을에 내리는 눈이
내 살고 있는 우듬지로 내리고 있다
아직 젊은 그 사내의 푸른 이마에 삼월의 눈이 온다
"봄을 바라고 서 있는 사나이의 관자놀이에
새로 돋은 정맥(靜脈)이
바르르 떤다."*
김춘수 시인의 업과 한이 쉬
떠나지 못한 채 취기 가득한 모습으로 맴돌아
내 아파트에까지 삼월의 눈이 오는 것인가
우울증이 도져 봄을 맞기 싫은 동면의 시샘인가
샤갈의 마을에서 보았던 아직
젊은 그 사내의 푸른 이마가 걸어온다
반복되는 일상의 수레바퀴쯤으로 여긴
춘삼월(春三月) 눈은 복숭아 꽃잎 같은 살을 펼치고 있다
오늘만큼은 풍경 속 몽상에 젖은 채
샤갈의 마을에 내리는 눈을 맞으며
나도 그를 만나고 싶다.

* 김춘수의 「샤갈의 마을에 내리는 눈」에서 인용.

The Snow in March

The snow in Chagall's town is falling in
Woodunji where I live
On the blue forehead of a young man
the March snow falls
"The new vein stemming from the temple of a man who
stands waiting for the spring
trembles."
Perhaps the karma of the poet Kim Chunsu spins around us,
hesitating to leave, and pushes the snow of March
even to my apartment
Is it the jealousy of winter that doesn't welcome the spring
The blue forehead of the young man in Chagall's town
is coming forward
The snow of March spreads her peach blossom like body
pink
Especially today
I'd like to meet him in the falling snow from Chagall's town
in my daydream

핫라인 통신

난 신기루 불꽃 같은 사랑의 매파, 별똥별 떨어지는 밤하늘의 낙화 폭죽 터트리는 불꽃놀이, 불똥 떨어지는 저 꽃잎 경포대 홍장암 바라보며 길게 허리 펴던 그날 밤하늘에 쏘아대던 허난설헌의 한 지천으로 내려앉고 가방끈 긴 사촌은 목동에서 논술을 지도하고 「오자히르」*, 자히르 당신을 찾아가건만 원준 할머니는 문중 산 걱정으로 잔뜩 겁먹은 얼굴로 흥얼거리고 또 한해를 넘겨야 하는 노파는 쭉정이 날개 파득일 힘도 없고 허리케인 같은 바람기둥이 될까 생각했고 그래서 생각해 보낼 수밖에 없는 당신이 기억되고 사르트르 헤세 보들레르, 문득 토우넬라의 백조 아무 생각나지 않는 가위에 눌린 백조.

* 파울로 코엘료의 소설, 아랍어로 '자히르(Zahir)는 눈에 보이며, 현존하는, 감지될 수밖에 없는 어떤 것으로, 일단 맞닥뜨리게 되면 조금씩 우리의 사고를 점령해, 어떤 것에도 집중할 수 없게 만들어 버리는 어떤 대상 혹은 존재를 말한다.

Hot Line Communication

I'm a mirage match maker of flaming love the fallen blossoms of the night sky where meteors fall, fireworks with fire crackers, the falling petals of flame. I stretch looking at Hongjang pavilion. That day the burning heart of Heonanseolheon is falling down all over the place. My cousin with higher education teaches at an institution at Mokdong. 「Oh Zahir」 I go to find you but Wonjun's grandma murmurs, worrying about her ancestors' mountains. The old woman has no energy to flapp her withered wings to survive another year. I think I'd like to be a hurricane. As a result I remember you whom I had to send away after deep thought. Sartre, Hesse, Baudelaire, Townella's swan. The swan troubled by a dim nightmare.

봄

택배가 왔네요. 어머니 같은 한국의 야생화, 가득 꽃으로 걸어 왔네요. 간밤에 꿈결로 속삭이긴 했지만 이렇게 빨리 올 줄 몰랐네요. 물론 내 바람처럼 바쁜 일손 멈추고 누구도 모르는 수신자도 발신자도 없는 극비로 부쳤네요. 흐드러진 봄꽃들은 연둣빛 창가에서 하늘거리네요. 개나리, 진달래, 홍매화 얘네들도 함께 마실 왔네요. 아름답네요. 세상 속 어깨 들썩이며 춤추고 있네요. 자연은 누구도 흉내 낼 수 없는 것 살 만한 세상이라고 그렇게 말하고 싶네요. 이른 아침 택배 한 상자 봄으로 받고 보니 마음 환해지네요.

Spring

A package is delivered. The Korean wild flowers resembling Mother. They come on foot. Last night we whispered in a dream, but I didn't expect such an early arrival. To my wish they sent it secretly, without any addresser and any addressee, stopping their busy work. The splendid spring flowers are swaying by the light green window. Forsythia, azalea and red plum blossom. They also come out to play. Beautiful. They are moving their shoulders up and down. Nothing can imitate nature. It's a wonderful world to live in, isn't it? The early morning delivery of spring brightens my heart.

아픈 손가락

86세 김 할머니 묘지는 볕 바른 평평한
산정에 세워지다
몸피가 가랑잎처럼 버석한 그녀,
가시박인 손가락 때문 검게 타들어 간 심장
위장에 생긴 종양은 화기로 자랐고
산소 같은 고명딸 깁스한 채 찾아들던 날
종양은 점점 크게 자리 잡았다
자존심으로 버티어 낸 가슴에 들이찬 화기는
용 비늘처럼 빛나던 그녀의 패기를 일순간 삼켜 버리고
오랜 시간 속 견디어 낸 마음 밭은
쑥대밭으로 갈아 뭉개지다
개울물 같은 음성, 회초리로 내리치던 독설,
두 번 보려 해도 볼 수 없고 들을 수조차 없다
8월의 태양은 금이 갔다
할머니의 뼈들이 가루 되어 내린다
가랑잎보다 가벼운
마르고 뒤틀어진 절절한 뼈들이
한 줌 재로

부서져 내린다. 김 할머니의 주검 앞에 진눈깨비로 내린다.
43년 만의 찾아온 폭염의 열대야
혹서의 젖은 어깨는 무게에 눌려 펑펑 휘날리고
이승에서의 지독한 외로움 방울방울 눈물 달고
걸어나간다
피의 봉분으로 솟았던 입
수의로 가려진 채 김 할머니 이방인 되어
걸어나간다 아 가여운 내 어머니

A Sore Finger

The tomb of 86 year old grandma Kim was made
on a sunny flat hill top
Her body skin was like a withered leaf
Her heart burnt black due to a thorny finger
The tumor in her stomach grew a stifling sensation
When her only sine qua non daughter visited her wearing a cast
her tumor grew bigger and bigger. However
the stifling sensation in her chest endured by her self-esteem
swallows her aspiration, which glows like a dragon's scale;
her field of mind withstanding for a long time
is completely devastated
Her stream like voice
Her slanderous tongue, like a whip
We no longer see and hear them
The August sun is cracked
The powders of her bones fall

The thin and twisted bones, lighter than withered leaves,
fall as ashes
The bones fall as sleet before grandma Kim's corpse
The tropical night after 43 years
Her shoulders, soaked by the heat, flutter
Her severe loneliness in this world walks
forward holding tear drops
Her mouth of blood mound
Grandma Kim in shroud walks forward as a stranger
Oh poor Mother

문안의 여자 문밖의 여자

문안의 여자가 낭만이 있으면
푼수가 되고
문밖의 여자가 분위기 타면
소녀가 된다

문안의 여자와 의견이 틀리면
도저히 무식하여 못 살겠다고 하면서
문밖의 여자와 이야기하다 엇갈려도
똑똑하고 당차다고 한다

문안의 여자가 계절을 타면
팔자 좋은 소리 한다고 핀잔주면서
문밖의 여자가 외롭다고 하면
애처로워 마음 아리다고 주접까지 떤다

문안의 여자가 화장하고 있으면
술집 여자 같다고 무안 주면서
문밖의 여자는 진한 화장까지 해도

세련되고 우아하다면서 칭찬까지 한다

문안의 여자가 생일이라면
집구석에서 뭔 놈의 생일이냐고 하고
문밖의 여자가 생일이라고 하면
꽃다발 들고 선물까지 준비하여 허겁지겁 달려가는
오지랖 넓은 남정네들…

문밖의 여자는 순간이지만
문안의 여자는 평생인 것을
어찌 모르는가

The Woman Inside The Woman Outside

When the woman inside is romantic
she is regarded as an idiot. However,
when the woman outside is in a romantic atmosphere
she is treated like a girl

When the woman inside has a different opinion
she becomes ignorant. However,
the different thinking of the woman outside is
viewed like an intellectual

When the woman inside is a little bent by the weather
she's scolded for having a fever pitch. However,
when the woman outside says she's lonely
she's consoled passionately

When the woman inside puts on make up
she's told she's like a bar girl. However,
the heavy make up of the woman outside is

complimented for her elegance

The birthday of the woman inside is
ignored. However,
the birthday of the woman outside is
celebrated with men holding a gift and a bouquet
What nosy men they are...

How come they don't know
the woman outside is just a joy of a moment but
the woman inside is a lifelong treasure?

단풍

가을 햇살 한 움큼
주머니에 챙겨
꾹
꾹 눌러 넣는다

가슴 속 전부를 태우고도
모자라
온산을 불태우고
강변에서 훌쩍 건너뛰어
숲 속 전체에 불을 질렀다

강변 주위엔
손가락 나뭇잎들이
붉은 그네를 탄다

Autumn Leaves

A handful of autumn sunlight
Firmly
Firmly I push it
into the pocket

After burning all my heart
Even the mountain
across the riverside
And all the forest

Along the riverside
Finger shaped leaves sit in a red swing

비 rain

Audi 문을 열고 들어서다
Audio에선 좋아하는 가수가 춤을 추고
와이퍼가
유리창을 뛰어다니고
창밖 지난날 흔적이
파랗게 질린 얼굴로 호외를 뿌린다
공치사하고픈 나
내가 나를 향해 말한다
둘이서 소화해야 할
너를 찾아
문안으로 들어섰을 때
그래도 따습게 맞아준
네 큰 손이 빗물을 길게 쓸어내리고
쉽게 마르지 않는 사연,
무서운 기세로 퍼붓던 비
목덜미를 향해 적신다

생각하는 사람 로댕*의

심장 뛰는 소리가 only you 창에 매달려 어려운 길
돌아왔음을 아는지 수천수만 개로 흩어져
한(恨) 품은 섬광으로 번쩍이다
pm 3:00 비 비 비
이제 멈춰야 할 시간
유리창을 거칠게 후려치는 손에
입맞춤한 손가락이
이정표를 클릭해도
물음표만 던지다

The Rain

I open the door of the Audi
My favorite singer dances on the radio
The wiper is running on the wind-shield
The past trace whose face is pale
handouts extras
To sing my own praise I say to myself
When I come inside to look for you whom
both of us should understand
you welcome me wiping the rain drops
The endless stories,
The pouring rain
It points at my neck

The heart beat of Rodin's Le Penseur
hangs on the wind shield and then
sparkles holding its grudge
3 P.M. Rain Rain Rain
It's time to stop

The hands of rain, flapping the windscreen hard,
cast a question mark
ignoring the clicked mile post

제 4 부

목관 악기의 일기

The Diary of a Brass

달 moon

너에게 걸어 들어가는 나 아무도 발견 못 했다

어디에선가 바라보는 불빛
이미 졸고 미처 달아나지 못한 어둠
스위치를 올리자 후다닥 흩어지는 먼지처럼
잠자던 네가 일어섰다
창밖으로 비친 도시의 실루엣 한없이 붉다
문밖 하나의 그림자 문을 연 순간
물밑으로 몸을 숨긴 구석진 삶이
젖은 습기를 닦아내고 있다

밤하늘에 흐린 얼굴 가슴으로 버티어 내고 있다

The Moon

No one notices me walking into you

The light shared by unseen eyes
The darkness losing a chance of escape
Upon turning on the switch
you wake up like a scattering dust
The silhouette of a city on the window is immensely red
At the moment a shadow outside opens the door
a marginal life who hides his body under water
wipes moisture

You endure your vague face darkened by the night sky
with the light of your heart, shared but unseen

동해가는 길 1
—초복

그녀 생각하며 가는 길
이야기꽃 마음속에 담고
좋아하시는 삼계탕 포장해 들고 간다

그녀 보러
버스 타고 가는 길
내 서러움에 울컥하기도 하고
자유로움에 행복해하기도 하다

짧디짧은 입속으로 무엇인가
넣어 드리고 싶어
우유 치즈 잣
요것저것 사 본다

과일도 그다지
좋아하시는 것 없고
즐겨 하시는 것이라곤 생선회밖에 없으니
나는 또 회를 뜬다

사람들과
친구들과
회를 먹을 때마다
그녀가 생각난다

The Road to Donghae 1
—The First Day of Dog Days

Thinking of her
I put the topic of conversation into my heart on my way to her
holding her favorite ginseng chicken soup

In a bus to see her
I fall into a sadness due to my sorrow
Also, I am happy in my freedom

As she is so picky
I try to pick up various things to feed her
Milk, cheese, pine nuts

She barely likes fruit
As her favorite is raw fish
I buy it again

Whenever I eat raw fish

with my friends or

with my fellow

I think of her

동해 가는 길 4

누구를 만난다는 것은
누구를 볼 수 있다는 것은
저 꽃들이 핀 것처럼 행복하다
고향으로 품어주던
영혼의 둥지였던
사랑과 영혼을 동시에 건네주었던
항시 그 자리에 서 있던 당신

때로는
건네주다가
때로는
순간 앗아 가버린

이제 나 영혼도 둥지도 없는 그리워하는 사람이 되어
쓸쓸히 쓸쓸히 이 길을 가는구나

창밖으로 휙휙 지나가는 풍경들이
하나도 아름답지 않은

저 힘찬 동해의 수평선처럼
고독하기만 하여서 나 저무는 노을이 되어
홀로 지고 있다네

The Road to Donghae 4

To meet somebody and
to see somebody is
as happy as those bloomed flowers
You used to embrace me as a hometown
You, the home of my spirit
Standing always in the same place
you give me love and soul

Sometimes
you give
Sometimes
you rob

Now not having a spirit and a net
I become a person of yearning and go on my way home
despairingly, despairingly

As the sceneries out of the bus window

extend, like the horizon of the powerful East Sea, they aren't beautiful but lonely
I become a green flash and set all alone

갯나루의 봄

골목 그림이 쓸쓸하게 느껴지다
속초시 청호동 아바이마을 1076으로
발길이 닿았다

집단 촌락을 형성한 풍경 속
60년대의 변천사다
휴전선 가까운 바닷가, 작은 포구
자판기에서 막 빠져나온
해풍의 커피 한 잔 같은
자전거를 세우고 일출을
바라보는 아바이를 보다

함경도의 피난민이다
거친 숨소리로 먼저 와 있는
이 새벽
갈 곳 없다 나는,
저만치서 늙은 아바이가 갯배를 띄우고
파도의 건반을 누르고 있다.

The Spring at a Ferry

The alley's scene seems lonely to me
I get to 1076 Abai town, Cheonghodong, Sokcho

The scenery of a collective village
formed in the 1960s
At a small port near the truce line
I watch a man see the sunrise by his bike which
looks like a cup of sea breeze coffee,
humming from the vending machine

He is the refugee from Hamgyeong Province
Already dawn
I have no place to go
Far away an old man floats his boat and plays
the keyboard of waves

모래성의 전설

한 쌍의 비둘기 동쪽으로 창문을 낸 성벽을
언덕 위에 쌓았다
바람 한점 침범치 못하는 철옹성
그곳엔

복사꽃 피고
돛단배 떠 있는 푸른 바다와 나뭇잎 붉게
물든 들녘이 있었으며
함박눈 내리는 날도 있었다, 그러나

벽을 둔 사이가 높고
밀물이 끝없이 밀려와 금 가기 시작한 성벽
외투의 깃 세운 비둘기 날개 접고 밀물처럼 빠질 때
성은 부서졌다

무너진 모래성 밖,
식솔들은
바람을 맞는 사철나무가 되었다

비둘기 구구대는 마음속 허허로운 전설의 성터만
가슴 깊은 뿌리로 살고 있다

The Legend of a Sand Castle

A pair of pigeons build a fort with
a window to the east
The fortress, strong,
even bits of wind can't slice through

The peach blossoms bloom,
the blue sea with a floating sailer, the field with red leaves, and
the days of large flakes of snow are there; but

The space between the walls is high and
the fort is cracked by the swaying flood
When the pigeons slip away like an ebb folding their wings
the castle shatters

Outside the collapsed sand
members of the family
become the spindle trees against the wind

Only the legendary ruined castle site filled with pigeons' clucks
lives as a memory with a deep heart.

창窓

내 숨 같은 당신
보고 있나요
창가에는 꽃들이 천지사방 하늘거리며
웃고 있는데
잘 지내는지요
당신 얼굴 대신 사진틀 속 네모난 액자 속의 나
그것이 가끔 보고픈 당신 생각하는 창이란 것을
세차게 흔들던 바람 부는 강가에서
내 숨 같은 사람 보내고
"누가 내 방문을 열면 알겠지
둥근 시계 대신 걸려 있는
네모난 액자 하나
그것이 내가 유일하게 보는 창이란 것을."*

* 이기종 시인의 「창」에서 인용

The Window

My darling of my life
Are you looking out of the window?
By the window swaying flowers are smiling
all over the place
How is everything?
Instead of your face mine is in the square frame
That's the window where I think of you whom
I miss from time to time
At the windy river side
I send my darling of my life away
"If anybody opens my door, then he'll know
a square frame hung on the wall
instead of a round clock,
that is the only window I look out of."*

* Quotations from the 「The Window」 by Lee Gi-jong

목관악기의 일기

납골당 같은 서랍 속 베일을 벗으렵니다
지루한 그대의 아침에서 하루를 열고 문을 닫는 시간
잠시 고뇌와 방황의 늪에서 찰나에 불과한
순간의 반짝임은 행복 같은 것이었습니다

여기
소리치는 목소리 있습니다
조간을 읽고 화들짝 놀라는
안경 너머로 누군가 나를 훔쳐보는 이 있다는 것

함께라면
아마도 지금쯤 주검의 목관 악기로 울고 섰을 겁니다
놀라운 새 생명
그것은 당신 덕분입니다
당신의 체온 속에
들어 있다는 것 감사로 지켜주는 깊은 사랑
내 나이의 숫자는
당신의 깃에서 접었습니다

대책 없는 나목으로 홀로 앉은 그림자를 내려놓으렵니다
이제 벗으렵니다
지루한 베일을 벗으렵니다

The Diary of a Brass

I'd like to take off the veil in the drawer
similar to a charnel house
When I open your boring morning and
close the door of a day
the glitters of a moment from the mosses of agony and wander
were happiness

Here
is a shouting voice
There
is someone peeking at me over his glasses who
is frightened at the morning newspaper

If we were together
we might be standing as a crying woodwind of death
by now
The surprising new life

It owes to you
It is in your temperature. Your deep love of me
The number of my age is folded in your plumes

I'd like to put down the shadow
sitting alone defenselessly as a naked tree
I'd like to take off
I'd like to take off the boring veil

밥

무슨 재미로 세상을 사셨을까 몰라
무슨 낙으로 살기 위한 생을
삼키셨을까 몰라
죄 많은 불초여식
임종 못 지킨 불초여식
당신의 아픈 손가락 되어
심장 까맣게 타들어 간 숯 검댕이
저승길 떠나는 주검의 참상
차려진 49제 막제

살아생전 어머니처럼 웅크리고 앉아
꾸역꾸역
마른 밥을 삼킨다
목울대로 넘기지 못할 때
물 한 사발 떠 힘없이 물 말아 드시던,
80평생 사는 게 미안하신지
너 오라비 아들 "원준이(장손) 장가가는 거 보고 죽을란다"
그때까지만 참고 봐주면 안 되겠냐!!

백 년도 못다 낄 틀니로
살기 위해 씹던 밀기울 같은 어머니의 밥처럼,
꾸역꾸역 내 입으로 쑤셔 넣는 찬밥
한 덩이

Boiled Rice

I don't know what her joy of life was
I don't know what fun made her survive the struggle
Her guilty daughter
Her daughter who wasn't present at her deathbed
Her daughter who became her sore finger and
let her heart burn black
Her body ready for the other world
The last, 49th ritual service

I crouch like Mother and eat dried rice
one after another
When she couldn't swallow easily
she used to eat a bowl of rice in water feebly
Feeling sorry for her old age of 80
she said, "Can't you endure me until the wedding day of
your brother's first son Wonjun?"
Mother's rice was like bran
She chewed it with her false teeth that she couldn't use

until the age of 100

A spoonful of cold rice

I stuff it into my mouth against my will

이팝나무 꽃잎은 안다

가려진 커튼 사이
시간은 흐르고 등 뒤로
날카로운 시선 꽂히다

멍치를 헤집던 예리한 바늘
얼음의 칼처럼
차가운 자리
허둥대는 사실을 감추기 위함인가
물 위를 천천히 밟고 있다

식은땀 같은 것
정수리에 사정없이 꽂히는 혹서
합일점은 끝내 찾지 못한 채 중증의
장애를 멍에처럼 진다

목덜미 죄어 오는 뒤엉킨 그물
전신을 포획한다
무릎까지 차오른 담뱃재

희뿌연 연기가
투혼을 불태우며 줄달음치는
미쳐버린 그 여름날

이팝나무 같은 아이들의 얼굴이
바닥을 치고 있다

The Asian Fringe Blossoms Know

Between the hidden curtains
time flows and keen eyes are thrown on the back

A sharp needle poking the pit of the stomach
A cold place like the sword of ice
Is it for hiding the fluttering truth
It is stepping on the water slowly

Something like a cold sweat
The fierce heat stuck in the crown of the head
It comes under a severe obstacle of yoke
not finding the unity

The tangled nets, seizing the nape of the neck, capture
the whole body
The tobacco ashes covered beneath the knee
That crazy summer day when the hazy smoke is running
away inflaming its fighting spirit

The faces of the children like Asian Fringe are hitting the bottom

이 혜 숙
(Lee Hye-sook)

이혜숙 시인의 호는 재랑이고 강원도 삼척에서 태어나 동해서 자랐으며 강릉에서 36년을 살고 있다. 2001년 월간 〈문학공간〉으로 등단했다. 2002년 재능교육&도민일보가 공동주최하는 전국 시낭송대회에서 최우수상을 수상하여 시낭송가 자격증 획득하였으며, 강릉원주대학 시낭송 강사를 역임하였다. 시집으로 『별 강물위로 몸을 던지고』(문학마을), 『수족관 숭어』(시평사), 『두레박 길어 올리는 시간』(한강), 『문 안의 여자 문밖의 여자』(글나무)가 있다

She was born in Samcheok, raised in Donghae and has lived in Gangneung for 36 years
Her pen name is Jaeryang
She debuted as a poet from Poet's Space in 2001.
She got a poem reading certificate from a national poem reciting contest by Jaeneung Education & Domin Daily in 2002 and worked at Gangneung Wonju University as a poem reading instructor
Her Korean books: The Star, It Throws Herself Over the River
The Mullet in an Aquarium
The Time When I Draw Water With a Bucket
Her Korean-English book: The Woman Inside vs The Woman Outside
Award: The 8th Writer's Award from Gangwon Literature
HP: 010-2944-8756
E-mail: poetry55@hanmail.net

번역: 이영순(李榮順) 詩人
Translated by Lee Young-soon

이혜숙 한영(韓英)시집

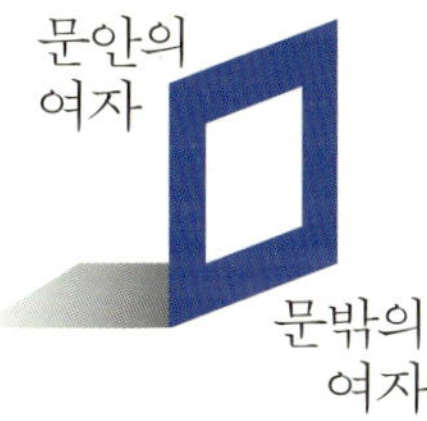

The Woman Inside The Woman Outside

저 자 | 이혜숙
발행자 | 오혜정
펴낸곳 | 글나무
서울시 중구 수표로 45. 비즈센터 905호
전 화 | 02)2272-6006
등 록 | 1988년 9월 9일(제301-1988-095)

2016년 3월 10일 초판 인쇄·발행

ISBN 978-89-91356-92-4 03810

값 10,000원

저자와 협의하여 인지를 생략합니다.